Th

Jamaican Drinks

Recipes

15 Authentic Mixed Beverage Recipes from Jamaica

By

Grace Barrington-Shaw

More books by Grace Barrington-Shaw:

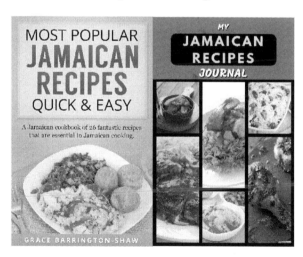

Disclaimer

All reasonable efforts have been made to provide accurate and error-free recipes within this book. These recipes are intended for use by persons possessing the appropriate technical skill, at their own discretion and risk. It is advisable that you take full note of the ingredients before mixing and use substitutes where necessary, to fit your dietary requirements.

Contents

Introduction

No meal is truly complete without a refreshing beverage to compliment. Jamaica has many beverages aside from the popular cocktails. There is a wonderful range of originally mixed drinks, for a variety of purposes, that can be enjoyed in a variety of settings.

In this recipe book, I celebrate the Jamaican mixed drinks that are loved throughout Jamaica and all over the world. Well known drink recipes which Jamaicans have passed down from generation to generation. Ask any Jamaican about the popular Sorrel, Irish Moss, Guinness Punch, Peanut Punch or Carrot Juice and they are likely to insist that you sample some that they have made immediately!

These drink recipes require Jamaicans to make use of locally available fruits, vegetables, nuts and other ingredients, to create some of the most delicious drink options in the Caribbean. Not only are they thirst quenching, but many of them also have noted health benefits. The recipes are highly adaptable, feel free to add your own ingredients to place your personal spin on these traditional favorites, or enjoy them in their original form. You'll be amazed at how simple these drinks are to mix and how great they taste.

FREE Bonuses

We have 3 **FREE** bonus recipe ebooks for your enjoyment!

- **Cookie Cookbook** 2134 recipes
- **Cake Cookbook** 2444 recipes
- **Mac and Cheese Cookbook** 103 recipes

Simply visit: **www.ffdrecipes.com** to get your **FREE** recipe ebooks.

You will also receive free exclusive access to our World Recipes Club, giving you FREE best-selling book offers, discounts and recipe ideas, delivered to your inbox regularly.

Sorrel

Sorrel is a drink that is traditionally enjoyed in Jamaica during the Christmas holidays, alongside Christmas cake and Christmas dinner. The sorrel plant is an annual plant which only blooms at a certain time of year, however since the flowers can be dried and stored, this drink can be enjoyed all year round, typically bottled and sold in supermarkets. It has a naturally tangy flavor and is deep red in color, although an alternative variety exists, bearing white or pinkish flowers, the deep red variety is the most abundant.

Serves 6 to 8 people

Ingredients

1 lb sorrel

2 to 4 ounces ginger root

8 cups water

Sugar to sweeten

Wine or rum (optional)

8 to 12 pimento seeds or 4 to 6 cloves

Preparation

1. Wash the sorrel well in water and add it to a stainless-steel vessel that has enough space to accommodate the water.

2. Remove the skin of the ginger by scraping it away, then crush and add to the container with the sorrel.

3. Add the pimento or cloves.

4. Boil the water then pour onto the contents of the container and steep for four to six hours or overnight.

5. Pour off the liquid through a strainer into another container and sweeten to desired taste. You can also add rum or wine at this point, if desired.

6. Serve chilled.

Guinness Stout Punch

This bitter, sweet and hearty milk-based drink is quite popular among Jamaican men. It is also called "Strong Back" as it is believed to add to a male's sexual prowess. There are several variations to the way it is made but this recipe provides the basic ingredients. You will find suggestions for additional ingredients to add at the end of the recipe.

Serves 1 or 2 people

Ingredients

1 regular bottle Guinness stout

4 oz sweetened condensed milk

½ tsp nutmeg

1 tsp cinnamon

1 whole beaten egg

Preparation

1. Add the beaten egg to the Guinness and condensed milk in a blender, then blend.

2. Pour the drink into a pitcher that is suitable for covering and add the nutmeg and cinnamon, mixing slightly.

3. Place in the refrigerator covered, chill and serve cold.

Useful Tip

To add to the richness and flavor of the punch you may also add some or all of the following: supligen, oatmeal, peanuts, and some white Overproof Jamaican rum. The oats may also be soaked in the Guinness prior to blending with the other ingredients.

Irish Moss

This seaweed was originally introduced to the Island by the Irish and is commonly found on rocks in Jamaica by the sea. Like Guinness punch, it is believed to increase stamina and is consumed by men and women alike. Some people even use it for its medicinal properties.

Serves 12 people

Ingredients

¾ lb Irish Moss

3 ounces gum Arabic or gum acacia

1 can condensed milk (alternatively use 6 ounces honey)

12 ounces sugar

5 ounces isinglass

5 ounces linseed

3 tbsps vanilla

5 quarts water

2 tbsps grated nutmeg

Preparation

1. Thoroughly wash the Irish Moss then soak in water overnight in the ratio two parts water to one-part moss. (You may also choose to cook the Irish Moss however it will take longer to soften when cooking if not soaked).

2. Add the water to the pot and allow to come to a boil.

3. Add the moss, gum arabic, linseed and isinglass and cook for forty-five minutes until all except the moss has dissolved.

4. Strain the liquid into a container, discard the moss and add the remaining ingredients

5. Mix well then return to boil for ten minutes more.

6. Cool and rest in the fridge for at least five hours before serving.

Jamaican Pine Drink

This drink is not your regular pineapple juice, it utilizes just the skin of the pineapple, providing a way for you to make use of and enjoy the whole fruit with minimal wastage. It is especially refreshing on a hot day and can be had with a noon meal or dinner.

Serves 4

Ingredients

Peel from a whole pineapple

1 ¼ cups sugar

6 limes

1 finger ginger

5 cups water

Preparation

1. Properly wash the pineapple peel in water, then boil with the ginger and five cups water for about ten minutes.

2. Let the water cool and then blend with skins until smooth.

3. Strain the mixture then add the squeezed limes and sweeten.

4. Add the rest of the ingredients and stir.

5. Serve cold after refrigeration or over ice.

Carrot Juice

Carrot juice is a drink that is an essential part of Jamaican Sunday dinners. It is traditionally sweetened with condensed milk and sometimes Dragon or Guinness stout is added. In more recent times, people have chosen to use sugar and lime as alternatives. This recipe is the traditional creamy version.

Serves 3 or 4 people

Ingredients

2 lbs chopped or baby carrots

4 cups water (more may be required)

1 tin condensed milk

½ tsp nutmeg

1 tsp vanilla

½ tsp fresh ginger

Rum or stout if desired

Preparation

1. Blend the carrots with most of the water and strain using cheesecloth. Discard the residue.

2. Add the other ingredients and mix well.

3. Place in refrigerator and serve chilled.

Jamaican Ginger Beer

Ginger beer is a beverage which packs quite a zing. Ginger has a characteristically harsh flavor making this a bold drink. The traditional way to prepare the drink is to grate the ginger however for ease, this recipe recommends blending. Regularly enjoyed as a cool beverage on an afternoon by the beach or riverside, on a sweltering day. Commercially it is sold in bars and restaurants and is always carbonated.

Serves 8 to 10 people

Ingredients

1 lb ginger root

4 limes

10 cups water

Sugar

2 cups carbonated water (if you prefer it fizzy)

Preparation

1. Wash the ginger well, cut into smaller pieces and puree in the blender with two cups of the water.

2. Pour into a container and add the squeezed limes as well as the remaining water (which has been boiled and is still hot).

3. Steep covered for at least four hours or overnight at best.

4. Strain the contents and add the carbonated water if using.

5. Sweeten to desired taste and chill in the refrigerator until ready to serve.

Helpful Tip

If using carbonated water, use two cups less water.

Peanut Punch

This peanut-based drink is a great source of protein and is yet another energy building drink. Some people prefer to add oats and even Irish Moss to increase the potency. Alcoholic beverages in the form of a dark stout may also be added if desired. This recipe is a basic version of the punch and allows you to get creative.

Serves 4 people

Ingredients

8 ounces peanuts (roasted inside the shell)

5 cups water

1 tin condensed milk

½ teaspoon vanilla

½ teaspoon grated nutmeg

1 teaspoon honey

½ teaspoon cinnamon powder (optional)

Preparation

1. Shell the peanuts and place them in a blender with half the water.

2. Blend and gradually add the rest of the water until the mixture is well liquefied.

3. Pour the liquid into a jug and add the remaining ingredients, mixing well.

4. Refrigerate and serve cold.

Beetroot Juice

Beetroot juice can be made with or without milk and is commonly paired with carrots. This recipe demonstrates both variations of pure beetroot juice. One version makes use of raw vegetable while the other uses cooked. Either version can be had with lunch or dinner and is a great way to boost blood count.

Serves 1 to 2 people

Ingredients

1 beetroot (large)

1 lime

8 ounces water

1 slice of ginger

Honey or sugar to sweeten

Preparation

1. Wash the beetroot well, cut it into cubes and place into the blender with the ginger and water.

2. Squeeze the juice from the lime into the blender and also add the sweetener.

3. Blend all the contents until liquefied.

4. Strain the liquid into a container and adjust the taste to your liking if necessary.

5. Chill and serve.

Milk Version

Ingredients

7 beetroot, small

6 ounces evaporated milk or supligen

1 tsp vanilla

¼ tsp nutmeg

Condensed milk (to sweeten)

Water

Preparation

1. Wash the beetroots and boil them whole until they become soft (about ten minutes).

2. Pour the water off, immerse in cold water, strip the skin and cut each one into four pieces.

3. Blend with enough water to just cover the pieces then strain after blending.

4. Add the remaining ingredients to sweeten and flavor the drink, then chill before serving.

Sour Sop Juice

For some people, soursop juice is an acquired taste. As the name suggests, this fruit has a tart flavor. It is traditionally made sweetened with condensed milk and spruced up with spices however it is also enjoyed with added lime and sugar, providing a milk free drink. The use of lime is not entirely necessary due to the already sour nature of the fruit, so for the alternative version, sugar and water alone will suffice. This juice is commonly enjoyed with Sunday dinner and provides vitamins B and C.

Serves 6 people

Ingredients

1 ripe sour sop

1 tin condensed milk

1 teaspoon nutmeg

2 tablespoon vanilla

4 cups water

Preparation

1. Wash the sour sop and peel away the skin by hand.

2. In a bowl, use clean fingers to separate the pulp and remove the seeds.

3. Using a blender, blend the pulp along with the vanilla and nutmeg, adding water to achieve a very smooth puree.

4. Sweeten to desired taste and refrigerate to cool. Serve along with cubes of ice.

Rum Punch

Rum punch is a hit at Christmas time, get-togethers and also at Nine Nights (a Jamaican tradition where family and friends gather at the home of the deceased). The alcoholic content is very high and in times past, it was quite commonplace for tourists to take a sample of this drink back home with them after visiting Jamaica.

Serves 20 people

Ingredients

8 cups water

2 cups lime juice

6 cups strawberry syrup

4 cups Jamaican white overproof rum

Preparation

1. In a punch bowl or other large container, combine and mix all the ingredients.

2. Adjust the taste with water or rum as desired and serve over cubes of ice.

Tamarind Drink

Tamarind is a seasonal fruit however once the tree bears, the brown pods containing the tart pulp are available in abundance. Some people like to add a little baking soda to the drink to achieve a slightly fizzy sensation however this is more of a preference rather than a necessity.

Serves 8 to 10 people

Ingredients

2 cups ripe tamarind (removed from shells)

8 cups hot water

1 lime

Ginger (small piece)

Brown sugar

Preparation

1. Place the tamarind pulp into a large container and pour on half of the hot water. Leave for a minute.

2. Use a fork to crush the tamarind flesh to remove some of the pulp from the seed casing.

3. Add the grated ginger to the container, cover and leave to steep and cool.

4. After cooling, strain the liquid into a jug then add the remaining water and lime.

5. Sweeten to desired taste and refrigerate before serving.

Pumpkin Punch

Pumpkin punch is a drink that enables the use of pumpkin in a creative way. Pumpkin is a very common vegetable and if it grows in your region, the yield can be quite gratifying. Pumpkin does not survive for too long in the refrigerator, so this is an excellent way to minimize wastage while boosting your vitamin A supply.

Serves 2 to 4 people

Ingredients

1 lb pumpkin

½ bottle Guiness

1 can supligen

1 dash nutmeg

4 cups water

Preparation

1. Remove the skin and seeds from the pumpkin, cut into pieces, and boil in the water.

2. When the contents of the pot have cooled, place in a blender and blend until smooth with the remaining ingredients.

3. Serve with ice cubes.

Cherry Juice

Another seasonal fruit, the Jamaican cherry is high in vitamin C, higher than that of oranges. It makes a delicious and refreshing drink and can be had at breakfast, lunch or dinner time. It is best sweetened with granulated sugar as dark sugar can significantly alter the flavor.

Serves 2 to 3 people

Ingredients

3 lb ripened cherries

1 lime

8 cups water

½ cups granulated sugar

Preparation

1. Wash the cherries and place them in the blender with sufficient water, then blend.

2. Strain into a jug and add the squeezed lime and sugar.

3. Once the sugar has dissolved upon mixing, refrigerate before serving or pour over crushed ice to serve.

June Plum Juice

This summer time fruit is enjoyed green and ripe on the island, with a sprinkling of salt. In its ripened state, other Caribbean islands identify it as 'golden apple'. In Jamaica, the green June plum is used to make juice and it is well loved, so much so that you will now find it on supermarket shelves across various brands.

Serves 2 people

Ingredients

4 green June plums

1 finger of ginger (sliced)

1/3 cup granulated sugar

16 ounces water

Preparation

1. Wash, peel and cut away the flesh from the seeds of the plums.

2. Place all the flesh, ginger and water into a blender, then blend until smooth.

3. Strain the contents then add sugar to achieve desired taste.

4. Chill and serve.

Guava Juice

Guava is a fruit with a very strong flavor and smell, with many seeds. The flesh of the fruit may either be yellow or pink. It is also used to make quite a delicious jam. The pink variety is more commonly used for juices, as the flesh tends to be quite tart, with the yellow part of the fruit being sweeter. Either variety however, is suitable for making the juice.

Serves 4 people

Ingredients

6 ripe guavas

4 cups Water

1 tablespoon ground ginger or 1 finger ginger

Sugar

Preparation

1. Wash, peel and cut the guavas into smaller pieces.

2. Blend them along with the ginger then strain into a jug to remove the seeds.

3. Sweeten to desired taste then serve after chilling.

Conclusion

As you can see, Jamaican drinks are so much more than simply cocktails. They are wonderfully crafted fruitful blends with the flavors and flexibility to suit your personal taste and even to suit your dietary needs. I hope these popular recipes have introduced you to the wonderful Jamaican beverage possibilities. If you are familiar with these drinks, then you will have re-kindled your love for these special beverages.

Throughout all these recipes the guiding principle is the same; if it ripens, it can be made into a juice! I hope you have enjoyed these simple to make drink recipes and will not hesitate to share these authentic Jamaican flavors with family and friends.

Why not add some great tasting Caribbean cocktail recipes by grabbing a copy of my other book; **Cocktails Cookbook**

Just a reminder…don't forget to visit **www.ffdrecipes.com** for your FREE bonus cookbooks and to get exclusive access to our VIP World Recipes Club, which provides FREE book offers, discounts and recipe ideas!

Thank you.

Measurements & Conversions

US to Metric Corresponding Measures

Metric	Imperial
3 teaspoons	1 tablespoon
1 tablespoon	1/16 cup
2 tablespoons	1/8 cup
2 tablespoons + 2 teaspoons	1/6 cup
4 tablespoons	1/4 cup
5 tablespoons + 1 teaspoon	1/3 cup
6 tablespoons	3/8 cup
8 tablespoons	1/2 cup

10 tablespoons + 2 teaspoons	2/3 cup
12 tablespoons	3/4 cup
16 tablespoons	1 cup
48 teaspoons	1 cup
8 fluid ounces (fl oz)	1 cup
1 pint	2 cups
1 quart	2 pints
1 quart	4 cups
1 gallon (gal)	4 quarts
1 cubic centimeter (cc)	1 milliliter (ml)
2.54 centimeters (cm)	1 inch (in)
1 pound (lb)	16 ounces (oz)

Liquid to Volume

Metric	Imperial
15ml	1 tbsp
55 ml	2 fl oz
75 ml	3 fl oz
150 ml	5 fl oz (¼ pint)
275 ml	10 fl oz (½ pint)
570 ml	1 pint
725 ml	1 ¼ pints
1 litre	1 ¾ pints
1.2 litres	2 pints
1.5 litres	2½ pints
2.25 litres	4 pints

Weight Conversion

Metric	Imperial
10 g	½ oz
20 g	¾ oz
25 g	1 oz
40 g	1½ oz
50 g	2 oz
60 g	2½ oz
75 g	3 oz
110 g	4 oz
125 g	4½ oz
150 g	5 oz
175 g	6 oz
200 g	7 oz
225 g	8 oz
250 g	9 oz
275 g	10 oz

350 g	12 oz
450 g	1 lb
700 g	1 lb 8 oz
900 g	2 lb
1.35 kg	3 lb

G

Abbreviations

Abbreviation	Description
tsp	teaspoon
Tbsp	tablespoon
c	cup
pt	pint
qt	quart
gal	gallon
wt	weight
oz	ounce
lb	pound
g	gram
kg	kilogram
vol	volume

ml	milliliter
l	liter
fl oz	fluid ounce

Made in United States
Troutdale, OR
10/27/2023

14079414R10024